The
BOOK
of
SERVICES

Containing the
General Services of the Church
Adopted by the 1984 General Conference

The United Methodist Church

The United Methodist Publishing House
Nashville

THE BOOK OF SERVICES

Copyright © 1985 by The United Methodist Publishing House

Second Printing 1986

All rights reserved.
No part of this work may be reproduced or transmitted in any form or by any means, electronic or mechanical, including photocopying and recording, or by any information storage or retrieval system, except as may be expressly permitted by the 1976 Copyright Act or in writing from the publisher. Requests for permission should be addressed in writing to Abingdon Press, 201 8th Avenue South, Nashville, TN 37202.

This book is printed on acid-free paper.

ISBN 0-687-03627-5

MANUFACTURED BY THE PARTHENON PRESS AT
NASHVILLE, TENNESSEE, UNITED STATES OF AMERICA

Contents

Preface

These General Services were adopted into the Ritual of The United Methodist Church by the 1984 General Conference after undergoing the most extensive process of development and testing in the history of our Ritual.

When The United Methodist Church was formed in 1968, *The Book of Discipline* (¶1388) provided that "the Ritual of the Church is that contained in the *Book of Ritual* of The Evangelical United Brethren Church, 1959, and *The Book of Worship for Church and Home* of The Methodist Church." *An Ordinal* (ordination and consecration services for deacons, elders, and bishops) was added to the Ritual by action of the 1980 General Conference.

It quickly became apparent after 1968 that the new United Methodist Church needed supplemental worship resources that would provide alternatives that more fully reflected developments in the contemporary ecumenical church. The 1970 special session of General Conference authorized the Commission on Worship to begin work in this area. The General Conferences of 1972 and 1976 authorized the Board of Discipleship, as successor to the Commission on Worship, to continue this work. Any hasty action to produce a United Methodist Ritual was avoided out of a strong desire for the most careful and extensive process of development, testing, and evaluation.

The first of the new services to appear was *The Sacrament of the Lord's Supper: An Alternate Text 1972*, which sold over two million copies prior to its revision in 1980. *Word and Table: A Basic Pattern of Sunday Worship for United Methodists*, published in 1976, adapted the same general order of worship for use on every Sunday, whether or not there was Communion, and provided an introduction and commentary. This same book also introduced the new ecumenical calendar and lectionary, which were more fully presented in *Seasons of the Gospel: Resources for the Christian Year* (1979). The other general services published with introduction and commentary included *A Service of Baptism, Confirmation, and Renewal* (1976), *A Service of Christian Marriage* (1979), and *A Service of Death and Resurrection* (1979).

Each of these services was written by one or more well-known liturgical writers who worked closely with an editorial task force representing various areas of expertise in the field. Each service was then carefully examined and criticized by the entire elected membership of the Section on Worship of the Board of Discipleship, who usually sent the manuscript back to the writer(s) and task force several times before finally approving it. Sometimes outside evaluations were secured during this process. These services were published with the invitation for those who used them to give their evaluation and suggestions. They were widely used throughout United Methodism, and as a result a wealth of helpful responses was received. The services were also reviewed and in many cases used by liturgical scholars, pastors, and congregations of other denominations. Suggestions from their perspectives were most helpful.

In the light of all these suggestions the service texts were revised and published in the booklet *We Gather Together* (1980). These revised services were commended by the 1980 General Conference to local churches for trial use, and the Board of Discipleship was instructed to revise them in the light of this trial use and submit them to the 1984 General Conference for adoption into the Ritual of the Church.

During the past quadrennium another large quantity of helpful criticism and suggestions was received from local churches and from expert reviews both in our denomination and ecumenically. Particular help in the revision process was given by a panel of consultants who worked with the section staff and by the elected members of the Section on Worship.

Special care has been given to test the suitability of the Ritual in ethnic minority local churches. These services have been tested and evaluated in selected Black congregations, and the suggestions received have been most helpful. A Spanish language version with Hispanic cultural adaptations was published in 1981 and was approved by the 1984 General Conference, in revised form as edited by the Rev. Hugo Lopez with the aid of Hispanic consultants. A Korean version with cultural adaptations is being edited by the Rev. Sang E. Chun with the aid of Korean consultants and should be ready soon. A Japanese version of the Sunday Service has been published, and Japanese and Chinese versions of the General Services are under development. It is hoped that other Asian American and Native American versions can be developed as soon as possible. The cultural adaptations made in each case are being studied with a view to enriching all versions of the General Services by multicthnic contributions.

These General Services have been revised in the light of all these suggestions and contributions.

It is hoped that they will serve well the needs of United Methodist churches and also that criticisms and suggestions will continue. In this connection several understandings are important:

1. Adoption of these General Services into the Ritual of the Church in no way takes away the status of the existing Ritual of the Church (Methodist and Evangelical United Brethren) or discourages its use. Rather, by giving all three sets of General Services a place in the Ritual of the Church, a wide choice is being offered the congregations of our diverse denomination.

2. The various General Services are designed for maximum flexibility, so that with appropriate adaptations they can be used in a variety of situations. United Methodist local churches range from very large to very small in

membership, from very formal to very informal in worship style, from print oriented to orally oriented, and with a wide variety of ethnic and cultural heritages. Even so, there will be situations where adaptations are called for in a particular situation that are not explicitly provided for in the services themselves. In such cases it is hoped that those planning and leading worship will know that they have Christian liberty to meet the pastoral needs of their congregations.

3. Inevitably these services contain compromises at points where United Methodists are not of one mind. One especially difficult area throughout the years during which these services have been developed has been that of the tension between traditional and inclusive language. It has been the basic intention throughout the development process to avoid language that discriminates against women, against any racial or ethnic community, or against persons with handicapping conditions. Two particular guiding principles in this connection have been (a) not to use masculine language to refer to people in general, and (b) to seek a balanced diversity of scriptural imagery in addressing or referring to God. In practice, however, there have been frequent disagreements about particular usages. Many active participants in the development process would have pre-ferred wording different from that which now appears. These services as they stand represent the best resolution possible at this time. Those using these services may from time to time wish to change particular words deemed objectionable, and they should be assured of their freedom to do so.

4. This diversity should not obscure our fundamental unity in Christ and in historic Christianity. We stand on the fourfold authority of Scripture, tradition, experience, and reason—with Scripture primary. These services seek to avoid anything faddish or idiosyncratic. They represent an earnest attempt to heed Wesley's admonition that our worship "follow the Scriptures and the primitive Church," while at the same time speaking to the condition of contemporary

United Methodists. They represent an attempt to incorporate both the historic and ecumenical witness of the church and also the distinctive gifts that our United Methodist heritage enables us to contribute to the universal church.

May these services be used to the glory of God and the proclamation of the gospel of Jesus Christ.

Members of the Section on Worship: Stan DePano (chairperson), George W. Watson Sr. (vice chairperson), D. S. Dharmapalan (secretary), Bishop George W. Bashore, Donald Bueg, Carole Cotton-Winn, Melissa Lynn Ives, J. Sue Kana-Mackey, Merwin Kurtz, Mary Penn, Luis Sotomayor, Sharon Spieth, and Langill Watson.

Representing the Fellowship of United Methodists in Worship, Music and Other Arts: Janet Lee (president) and Patty Evans (executive secretary-treasurer), replaced in 1983 by Robert Bennett (president) and Jerry Henry (executive secretary-treasurer).

Staff of the Section on Worship: Ezra Earl Jones (general secretary), Noé E. Gonzales (associate general secretary), Hoyt L. Hickman (assistant general secretary and editor of the General Services), Richard L. Eslinger, Barbara P. García, and Judy L. Lochr.

Consultants for the General Services: Don E. Saliers, Gail Ramshaw-Schmidt, Laurence H. Stookey, James F. White, Susan J. White, and William H. Willimon.

Concerning Services of Word and Table

Flexibility is a necessity for all orders of worship in our day. They must be adaptable to the differing needs and circumstances in which diverse congregations worship.

One order of worship for the proclamation of God's Word and the celebration of the Lord's Supper is presented here. It is designed to express the historical and theological bases that give integrity to Christian worship. This order of worship is printed in several formats to show how it can be adapted to different situations, but in its essentials it is one order.

A Basic Pattern of Worship and *An Outline of Sunday Worship* are intended to make plain the structure of the order.

An Order of Sunday Worship expands upon the outline and can be used in the preparation of services conducted by announcement or by use of a bulletin. *Alternative Acts of Worship,* though not part of the General Services, should be published with *An Order of Sunday Worship* to illustrate the variety of texts that can be used with it.

For congregations that prefer to use a standard printed text, *A Service of Word and Table* (Complete Text) can be used instead of a bulletin. It is proposed that it be made available separately in an eight-page leaflet that can be pasted inside the back cover of hymnals.

The Lord's Supper (Brief Text) is intended to be employed in congregations that prefer to use a bulletin or be led by announcement during the Service of the Word but use a printed text during the Service of the Table. It will also appeal to those congregations that prefer a brief text with opportunity for interpolations by the minister. This brief text can also be used in home or other informal services.

The Lord's Supper (Minimum Text) is intended for use with the sick and shut-in and in other situations where brevity is essential and where the ability of persons to make verbal responses may, in varying degrees, be limited.

A selection of alternative texts for various acts of worship in this order follows. The *Thanksgiving and Communion* section of *An Order of Sunday Worship* is to be published as a bulletin insert, to be used with a revised edition of *At the Lord's Table*. That book of Communion resources will be essential for the variation of the service through the days, seasons, and special events of the Christian Year and life.

A Basic Pattern of Worship

The Entrance

The people come together in the Lord's name. There may be greetings, music and song, prayer and praise.

Proclamation and Response

The Scriptures are opened to the people through the reading of lessons, preaching, witnessing, music, or other arts and media. Interspersed may be psalms, anthems, and hymns. Responses to God's Word include acts of commitment and faith with offerings of concerns, prayers, gifts, and service for the world and for one another.

Thanksgiving and Communion

In services with Communion, the actions of Jesus in the Upper Room are reenacted:
    taking the bread and cup,
    giving thanks over the bread and cup,
    breaking the bread, and
    giving the bread and cup.

In services without Communion, thanks are given for God's mighty acts in Jesus Christ.

Sending Forth

The people are sent into ministry with the Lord's blessing.

An Outline of Sunday Worship

Gathering

Greeting

Hymn of Praise

Prayer of the Day,
    Confession and Pardon,
    and/or Litany

[Act of Praise]

[Prayer for Illumination]

Scripture Lesson

[Psalm]

[Scripture Lesson]

Hymn or Song

Gospel Lesson

Sermon

Response to the Word

Concerns and Prayers

[Confession and Pardon]

The Peace

Offering

With Communion or	*Without Communion*
Taking the Bread and Cup	Prayer of Thanksgiving,
Great Thanksgiving	concluding with the
Breaking the Bread	Lord's Prayer
Giving the Bread and Cup	

Hymn or Song

Dismissal with Blessing

Going Forth

An Order of Sunday Worship

The Entrance

GATHERING

The people come together in the Lord's name. While they are gathering, one or more of the following may take place:
   Informal greetings, conversation, and fellowship
   Announcements and welcoming
   Rehearsal of music and other acts of worship
   Informal prayer, singing, testimony
   Quiet meditation and private prayer
   Organ or other instrumental music

GREETING

The leader greets the people in the Lord's name, declaring that the Lord is present and empowers our worship. The people may respond.

HYMN OF PRAISE

The leader and people greet the Lord with praise. If the hymn is a processional or entrance song, it may precede the Greeting.

OPENING PRAYER(S)

This may be one or more of the following:
   Prayer of the Day
   Confession and Pardon
   Litany

[ACT OF PRAISE]

"Glory to God in the Highest," a psalm, an anthem, or some other act of praise may be sung or said.

Proclamation and Response

[PRAYER FOR ILLUMINATION]

The blessing of the Holy Spirit is invoked upon the reading, preaching, hearing, and doing of the Word. If the preceding act of praise has been omitted, this prayer may be included in the opening prayer(s).

SCRIPTURE LESSON

[PSALM]

A psalm or psalm portion may be sung or spoken.

[SCRIPTURE LESSON]

HYMN OR SONG

A hymn or song related to the Scriptures of the day, or an alleluia, may be sung.

GOSPEL LESSON

SERMON

One or more of the Scripture lessons are interpreted.

RESPONSE TO THE WORD

Responses may include one or more of the following acts:

Hymn of Invitation or Response, which may follow an Invitation to Christian Discipleship.

Baptism, Confirmation, Reaffirmation of Faith, or other Reception of Members.

A Creed.

CONCERNS AND PRAYERS

Brief intercessions, petitions, and thanksgivings may be prayed by the leader, or spontaneously by members of the congregation. To each of these, all may make a common response, such as: "Lord, hear our prayer."

Or, a litany of intercession and petition may be prayed.

Or, a pastoral prayer may be offered.

At this or some other time during the service, persons so desiring may be invited to kneel for prayer at the Communion rail.

[CONFESSION AND PARDON]

When there has not been an act of confession and pardon earlier in the service, the minister calls the people to self-examination and confession, leads them in confession of sin, and declares God's pardon for those penitent.

THE PEACE

The people offer one another signs of reconciliation and love.

OFFERING

A hymn, psalm, or anthem may be sung as the offering is received.

If Holy Communion is to be celebrated, the bread and wine are brought by representatives of the people to the Lord's table with the other gifts, or uncovered if already in place.

A hymn, doxology, or other response may be sung as the gifts are brought to the Lord's table.

Thanksgiving and Communion

TAKING THE BREAD AND CUP

If Holy Communion is to be celebrated, the minister takes the bread and cup, and the bread and wine are prepared for the meal.

If Holy Communion is not to be celebrated, a prayer of thanksgiving and the Lord's Prayer follow. The pattern of the Great Thanksgiving may be followed, without reference to the Lord's Supper. A brief time of silence may be substituted for Breaking the Bread and Giving the Bread and Cup.

THE GREAT THANKSGIVING

The Lord be with you.

And also with you.

Lift up your hearts.

We lift them to the Lord.

Let us give thanks to the Lord our God.

It is right to give our thanks and praise.

The minister gives thanks appropriate to the occasion, remembering God's acts of salvation, and concludes:

And so,
with your people on earth
and all the company of heaven
we praise your name and join their unending hymn:

**Holy, holy, holy Lord, God of power and might,
heaven and earth are full of your glory.
Hosanna in the highest.
Blessed is he who comes in the name of the Lord.
Hosanna in the highest.**

The minister continues the thanksgiving. If Holy Communion is to be celebrated, the institution of the Lord's Supper is recalled. The minister concludes:

And so,
in remembrance of these your mighty acts
in Jesus Christ,
we offer ourselves in praise and thanksgiving
as a holy and living sacrifice,
in union with Christ's offering for us,
as we proclaim the mystery of faith.

Christ has died, Christ is risen, Christ will come again.

The minister then invokes the present work of the Holy Spirit and then praises the Trinity, concluding:

All honor and glory is yours, Almighty Father *(God)*
now and for ever.

Amen.

The Lord's Prayer is prayed in unison.

BREAKING THE BREAD

The minister breaks the bread in silence, or with appropriate words.

The minister then lifts the cup in silence, or with appropriate words.

GIVING THE BREAD AND CUP

The bread and wine are given to the people,
with these or other words being exchanged:

The body of Christ, given for you. **Amen.**

The blood of Christ, given for you. **Amen.**

The congregation sings hymns while the bread and cup are given.

When all have received, the Lord's table is put in order.

The minister or congregation may give thanks after Communion.

Sending Forth

HYMN OR SONG
DISMISSAL WITH BLESSING
GOING FORTH

There may be organ or other instrumental music. After informal greetings, conversation, and fellowship, the people go forth into ministry.

A Service of Word and Table (Complete Text)

The Entrance

GATHERING

GREETING

The grace of the Lord Jesus Christ be with you.

And also with you.

The risen Christ is with us.

Praise the Lord!

HYMN OF PRAISE

OPENING PRAYER

The following or a prayer of the day is offered:

**Almighty God,
to you all hearts are open, all desires known,
and from you no secrets are hidden.
Cleanse the thoughts of our hearts
by the inspiration of your Holy Spirit,
that we may perfectly love you,
and worthily magnify your holy Name,
through Christ our Lord.
Amen.**

[ACT OF PRAISE]

Proclamation and Response

PRAYER FOR ILLUMINATION

**Lord, open our hearts and minds
by the power of your Holy Spirit,
that, as the Scriptures are read
and your Word proclaimed,
we may hear with joy what you say to us today. Amen.**

SCRIPTURE LESSON

[PSALM] *May be sung or spoken.*

[SCRIPTURE LESSON]

HYMN OR SONG

GOSPEL LESSON

SERMON

RESPONSE TO THE WORD

Responses may include one or more of the following acts:

Hymn of Invitation or Response, which may follow an Invitation to Christian Discipleship.

Baptism, Confirmation, Reaffirmation of Faith, or other Reception of Members.

The following or another creed:

I believe in God, the Father almighty,
creator of heaven and earth.

I believe in Jesus Christ, his only Son, our Lord.
He was conceived by the power of the Holy Spirit
and born of the Virgin Mary.
He suffered under Pontius Pilate,
was crucified, died, and was buried.
He descended to the dead.
On the third day he rose again.
He ascended into heaven,
and is seated at the right hand of the Father.
He will come again to judge the living and the dead.

I believe in the Holy Spirit,
the holy catholic Church,
the communion of saints,
the forgiveness of sins,
the resurrection of the body,
and the life everlasting. Amen.

CONCERNS AND PRAYERS

Brief intercessions, petitions, and thanksgivings may be prayed by the leader, or spontaneously by members of the congregation. To each of these, all may make a common response, such as: "Lord, hear our prayer."

Or, a litany of intercession and petition may be prayed.

Or, a pastoral prayer may be offered.

CONFESSION AND PARDON

At Holy Communion:

Christ our Lord
invites to his table
all who love him,
who earnestly repent
of their sin
and seek to live in peace
with one another.
Therefore,
let us confess our sin
before God and
    one another.

At Other Services:

Christ our Lord
calls all who love him
earnestly to repent
of their sin
and live in peace
with one another.
Therefore,
let us confess our sin
before God and
one another.

**Merciful God,
we confess that often we have failed
to be an obedient church.
We have not done your will,
we have broken your law,
we have rebelled against your love,
we have not loved our neighbors, and
we have not heard the cry of the needy.
Forgive us, we pray.
Free us for joyful obedience,
through Jesus Christ our Lord.
Amen.**

All pray in silence.

Minister to people:
Hear the good news:
"Christ died for us while we were yet sinners;
that proves God's love toward us."
In the name of Jesus Christ, you are forgiven!

People to minister:
In the name of Jesus Christ, you are forgiven!

Minister and people:
Glory to God. Amen.

THE PEACE

Let us offer one another signs of reconciliation and love.

All exchange signs and words of God's peace.

OFFERING

As forgiven and reconciled people,
let us offer ourselves and our gifts to God.

A hymn, psalm, or anthem may be sung as the offering is received.

*If Holy Communion is to be celebrated, the bread and wine are
brought by representatives of the people to the Lord's table with the
other gifts, or uncovered if already in place.*

*A hymn, doxology, or other response may be sung as the gifts are
brought to the Lord's table.*

Thanksgiving and Communion

TAKING THE BREAD AND CUP

*If Holy Communion is to be celebrated, the minister takes the bread
and cup, and the bread and wine are prepared for the meal.*

*If Holy Communion is not to be celebrated, the words that pertain
only to Holy Communion, marked by a vertical line (|), are omitted
from the Great Thanksgiving.*

THE GREAT THANKSGIVING

The Lord be with you.

And also with you.

Lift up your hearts.

We lift them to the Lord.

Let us give thanks to the Lord our God.

It is right to give our thanks and praise.

It is right, and a good and joyful thing,
always and everywhere to give thanks to you,
Father Almighty, Creator of heaven and earth.
You formed us in your image
and breathed into us the breath of life.
When we turned away, and our love failed,
your love remained steadfast.
You delivered us from captivity,
made covenant to be our sovereign God,
and spoke to us through your prophets.
And so,
with your people on earth
and all the company of heaven
we praise your name and join their unending hymn:

**Holy, holy, holy Lord, God of power and might,
heaven and earth are full of your glory.
Hosanna in the highest.
Blessed is he who comes in the name of the Lord.
Hosanna in the highest.**

Holy are you, and blessed is your Son Jesus Christ.
Your Spirit anointed him
to preach good news to the poor,
to proclaim release to the captives
and recovering of sight to the blind,
to set at liberty those who are oppressed,
and to announce that the time had come

when you would save your people.
He healed the sick, fed the hungry,
and ate with sinners.

By the baptism
of his suffering, death, and resurrection.
you gave birth to your Church,
delivered us from slavery to sin and death,
and made with us a new covenant
by water and the Spirit.
When the Lord Jesus ascended,
he promised to be with us always,
in the power of your Word and Holy Spirit.

On the night in which he gave himself up for us
he took bread, gave thanks to you, broke the bread,
gave it to his disciples, and said:
"Take, eat; this is my body which is given for you.
Do this in remembrance of me."

When the supper was over he took the cup,
gave thanks to you, gave it to his disciples, and said:
"Drink from this, all of you;
this is my blood of the new covenant,
poured out for you and for many
for the forgiveness of sins.
Do this, as often as you drink it,
in remembrance of me."

And so,
in remembrance of these your mighty acts
in Jesus Christ,
we offer ourselves in praise and thanksgiving
as a holy and living sacrifice,
in union with Christ's offering for us,
as we proclaim the mystery of faith.

Christ has died, Christ is risen, Christ will come again.

Pour out your Holy Spirit on us, gathered here,
and on these gifts of bread and wine.

Make them be for us the body and blood of Christ,
that we may be for the world the body of Christ,
redeemed by his blood.

By your Spirit make us one with Christ,
one with each other,
and one in ministry to all the world,
until Christ comes in final victory
and we feast at his heavenly banquet.

Through your Son Jesus Christ,
with the Holy Spirit in your holy Church,
all honor and glory is yours, Almighty Father,
now and for ever.

Amen.

And now, with the confidence of children of God, let us pray:

**Our Father in heaven,
hallowed be your Name,
your kingdom come,
your will be done,
   on earth as in heaven.
Give us today our daily bread.
Forgive us our sins
as we forgive those who sin against us.
Save us from the time of trial,
and deliver us from evil.
For the kingdom, the power, and the glory are yours
now and for ever. Amen.**

BREAKING THE BREAD

The minister breaks the bread in silence, or while saying:

Because there is one loaf,
we, who are many, are one body,
for we all partake of the one loaf.
The bread which we break
is a sharing in the body of Christ.

The minister lifts the cup in silence, or while saying:

The cup over which we give thanks
is a sharing in the blood of Christ.

GIVING THE BREAD AND CUP

*The bread and wine are given to the people, with these or other
words being exchanged:*

The body of Christ, given for you. **Amen.**
The blood of Christ, given for you. **Amen.**

*The congregation sings hymns while the bread and cup are
given.*

When all have received, the Lord's table is put in order.

The following prayer is then offered by the minister or by all.

Eternal God, we give you thanks for this holy mystery
in which you have given yourself to us.
Grant that we may go into the world
in the strength of your Spirit,
to give ourselves for others,
in the name of Jesus Christ our Lord.
Amen.

Sending Forth

HYMN OR SONG

DISMISSAL WITH BLESSING

Go forth in peace.
The grace of the Lord Jesus Christ,
and the love of God,
and the communion of the Holy Spirit be with you all.
Amen.

GOING FORTH

The Lord's Supper (Brief Text)

The people gather in the Lord's name.
They offer prayer and praise.

The Scriptures are read and preached.
Responses of praise, faith, and prayer are offered.

The service continues as follows:

CONFESSION AND PARDON

Minister: Christ our Lord invites to his table all who love him, who earnestly repent of their sin and who seek to live in peace with one another. Therefore, let us confess our sin before God and one another.

Minister and people: **Merciful God, we confess that often we have failed to be an obedient church. We have not done your will, we have rebelled against your love, we have not loved our neighbors, and we have not heard the cry of the needy. Forgive us, we pray. Free us for joyful obedience, through Jesus Christ our Lord. Amen.**

All pray in silence.

Minister to people: Hear the good news: "Christ died for us while we were yet sinners; that proves God's love toward us." In the name of Jesus Christ, you are forgiven!

People to minister: **In the name of Jesus Christ, you are forgiven.**

Minister and people: **Glory to God. Amen.**

THE PEACE

Minister: Let us offer one another signs of reconciliation and love.

All exchange signs and words of God's peace.

OFFERING

Minister: As forgiven and reconciled people, let us offer ourselves and our gifts to God.

An offering may be received, during which a hymn, psalm, or anthem may be sung. The bread and wine are brought to the Lord's table with the other gifts, or uncovered if already in place.

TAKING OF THE BREAD AND CUP

The minister takes the bread and cup, and the bread and wine are prepared for the meal.

THE GREAT THANKSGIVING

The Lord be with you.

And also with you.

Lift up your hearts.

We lift them to the Lord.

Let us give thanks to the Lord our God.

It is right to give our thanks and praise.

It is right, and a good and joyful thing, always and everywhere to give thanks to you, Father Almighty, Creator of heaven and earth. . . . And so, with your people on earth and all the company of heaven we praise your name and join their unending hymn:

Holy, holy, holy Lord, God of power and might, heaven and earth are full of your glory. Hosanna in the highest. Blessed is he who comes in the name of the Lord. Hosanna in the highest.

Holy are you, and blessed is your son Jesus Christ. . . . By the baptism of his suffering, death, and resurrection you gave birth to your Church, delivered us from slavery to sin and death, and made with us a new covenant by water and the Spirit. . . .

On the night in which he gave himself up for us he took bread, gave thanks to you, broke the bread, gave it to his disciples, and said: "Take, eat; this is my body which is given for you. Do this in remembrance of me."

When the supper was over he took the cup, gave thanks to you, gave it to his disciples, and said: "Drink from this, all of you; for this is my blood of the new covenant, poured out for you and for many for the forgiveness of sins. Do this, as often as you drink it, in remembrance of me."

And so, in remembrance of these your mighty acts in Jesus Christ, we offer ourselves in praise and thanksgiving as a holy and living sacrifice, in union with Christ's offering for us, as we proclaim the mystery of faith.

Christ has died, Christ is risen, Christ will come again.

Pour out your Holy Spirit on us, gathered here, and on these gifts of bread and wine. Make them be for us the body and blood of Christ, that we may be for the world the body of Christ, redeemed by his blood. . . . By your Spirit make us one with Christ, one with each other, and one in ministry to all the world, until Christ comes in final victory, and we feast at his heavenly banquet.

Through your Son Jesus Christ, with the Holy Spirit in your holy Church, all honor and glory is yours, Almighty Father, now and for ever.

Amen.

And now, with the confidence of children of God, let us pray:

Our Father in heaven,
hallowed be your Name,
your kingdom come,
your will be done, on earth as in heaven.
Give us today our daily bread.
Forgive us our sins
  as we forgive those who sin against us.
Save us from the time of trial,
and deliver us from evil.
For the kingdom, the power, and the glory are yours,
now and forever. Amen.

BREAKING THE BREAD

The minister breaks the bread and then lifts the cup, in silence or with appropriate words.

GIVING THE BREAD AND CUP

The bread and wine are given to the people, with these or other words being exchanged:

The body of Christ, given for you. **Amen.**

The blood of Christ, given for you. **Amen.**

The congregation sings hymns while the bread and cup are given.

When all have received, the Lord's table is put in order.

The minister may then give thanks after Communion.

SENDING FORTH

A final hymn or song may be sung.

The minister dismisses the people with this blessing:

Go forth in peace. The grace of the Lord Jesus Christ, and the love of God, and the communion of the Holy Spirit be with you all. **Amen.**

The Lord's Supper (Minimum Text)

*The people come together
and exchange greetings in the Lord's name.*

*Scriptures are read and interpreted.
Prayer and praise are offered.*

The minister then gives this or some other suitable invitation:

Christ our Lord invites to his table all who love him and seek to grow into his likeness. Let us draw near with faith, make our humble confession, and prepare to receive this holy Sacrament.

Minister and people: **We do not presume to come to this your table, merciful Lord, trusting in our own goodness, but in your unfailing mercies. We are not worthy that you should receive us, but give your word and we shall be healed, through Jesus Christ our Lord. Amen.**

The minister may say: Hear the good news: "Christ died for us while we were yet sinners; that is proof of God's love toward us." In the name of Jesus Christ, you are forgiven!

All may exchange signs and words of God's peace.

The minister takes the bread and cup, prepares the bread and wine for the meal, and then prays the Great Thanksgiving as follows:

Lift up your heart(s) and give thanks to the Lord our God.

Father Almighty, Creator of heaven and earth, you made us in your image, to love and to be loved. When we turned away, and our love failed, your love remained steadfast. By the suffering, death, and resurrection of your only Son Jesus Christ you delivered us from slavery to sin and death and made with us a new covenant by water and the Spirit.

On the night in which he gave himself up for us he took bread, gave thanks to you, broke the bread, gave it to his disciples, and said: "Take, eat; this is my body which is given for you. Do this in remembrance of me."

When the supper was over he took the cup, gave thanks to you, gave it to his disciples, and said: "Drink from this, all of you; for this is my blood of the new covenant, poured out for you and for many for the forgiveness of sins. Do this, as often as you drink it, in remembrance of me."

And so, in remembrance of these your mighty acts in Jesus Christ, we offer ourselves in praise and thanksgiving as a holy and living sacrifice, in union with Christ's offering for us.

Pour out your Holy Spirit on us and on these gifts of bread and wine. Make them be for us the body and blood of Christ, that we may be for the world the body of Christ, redeemed by his blood.

By your Spirit make us one with Christ, one with each other, and one in ministry to all the world, until Christ comes in final victory, and we feast at his heavenly banquet.

Through your Son Jesus Christ, with the Holy Spirit in your holy Church, all honor and glory is yours, Almighty Father, now and for ever.

Amen.

And now, with the confidence of children of God, let us pray:

**Our Father in heaven,
hallowed be your Name,
your kingdom come,
your will be done, on earth as in heaven.
Give us today our daily bread.
Forgive us our sins
as we forgive those who sin against us.
Save us from the time of trial,
and deliver us from evil.
For the kingdom, the power, and the glory are yours,
now and for ever. Amen.**

The minister breaks the bread.

The bread and wine are given to the people,
with these or other words being exchanged:

The body of Christ, given for you. **Amen.**

The blood of Christ, given for you. **Amen.**

When all have received, the Lord's table is put in order.

The minister may then give thanks after Communion.

A final hymn or song may be sung.

The minister gives this final blessing:

The grace of the Lord Jesus Christ, and the love of God, and
the communion of the Holy Spirit be with you all. **Amen.**

Alternative Acts of Worship

Greetings

1

The grace of the Lord Jesus Christ be with you.

And also with you.

The risen Christ is with us.

Praise the Lord!

2

Grace and peace to you from God our Father
and the Lord Jesus Christ.

Amen.

The risen Christ is with us!

Praise the Lord!

3

The Lord be with you.

And also with you.

4

In the name of the Father, and of the Son,
and of the Holy Spirit.

Amen.

Opening Prayers

1 *(for use on any day)*

Almighty God, to you all hearts are open,
all desires known,
and from you no secrets are hidden.
Cleanse the thoughts of our hearts
by the inspiration of your Holy Spirit,
that we may perfectly love you,
and worthily magnify your holy Name,
through Christ our Lord. **Amen.**

2 *(for use on any day)*

Almighty God: you are constant for ever,
glorious in holiness, full of love and compassion,
abundant in grace and truth.
All your works and all your people praise you,
and your glory is revealed in Christ, our Savior.
Therefore, we praise you, Blessed and Holy Trinity,
One God, now and for ever. **Amen.**

3 *(for use on the Lord's Day)*

Almighty God,
by raising Jesus Christ your Son
you destroyed the power of sin and death
and opened to us abundant and eternal life.
Grant, we pray, on this the Lord's Day,
that, as we celebrate Christ's resurrection,
the power of your Word and Holy Spirit
will raise us up and renew our lives,
through Jesus Christ our Lord. **Amen.**

4 *(for use on the Lord's Day)*

God of all glory,
on this first day you began creation,
bringing light out of darkness.
On this first day you began your new creation,
raising Jesus Christ out of the darkness of death.
Grant that we,
the people you create by water and the Spirit,
may be transformed by your Word
and live in the light of the resurrection.
Through Jesus Christ our Lord. **Amen.**

5 *(for use on any day)*

In peace, let us pray to the Lord.
Lord, have mercy.
For the peace from above, and for our salvation,
let us pray to the Lord.

Lord, have mercy.

For the peace of the whole world,
for the well-being of the Church of God,
and for the unity of all,
let us pray to the Lord.   ·

Lord, have mercy.

For this house of prayer,
and for all who offer here their worship and praise,
let us pray to the Lord.

Lord, have mercy.

Help, save, comfort, and defend us, gracious Lord.

Amen.

Creeds

1   THE NICENE CREED

We believe in one God,
the Father, the Almighty,
maker of heaven and earth,
of all that is, seen and unseen.

We believe in one Lord, Jesus Christ,
the only Son of God,
eternally begotten of the Father,
God from God, Light from Light,
true God from true God,
begotten, not made,
of one Being with the Father.
Through him all things were made.
For us and for our salvation
he came down from heaven:
by the power of the Holy Spirit
he became incarnate from the Virgin Mary,
and was made human.
For our sake he was crucified under Pontius Pilate;

he suffered death and was buried.
On the third day he rose again
in accordance with the Scriptures;
he ascended into heaven
and is seated at the right hand of the Father.
He will come again in glory
to judge the living and the dead,
and his kingdom will have no end.

We believe in the Holy Spirit, the Lord, the giver of life,
who proceeds from the Father and the Son.
With the Father and the Son
he is worshiped and glorified.
He has spoken through the Prophets.
We believe in one holy catholic and apostolic Church:
We acknowledge one baptism
for the forgiveness of sins.
We look for the resurrection of the dead,
and the life of the world to come.
Amen.

2 THE APOSTLES' CREED

I believe in God, the Father Almighty,
creator of heaven and earth.

I believe in Jesus Christ, his only Son, our Lord.
He was conceived by the power of the Holy Spirit
and born of the Virgin Mary.
He suffered under Pontius Pilate,
was crucified, died, and was buried.
He descended to the dead.
On the third day he rose again.
He ascended into heaven,
and is seated at the right hand of the Father.
He will come again to judge the living and the dead.

I believe in the Holy Spirit,
the holy catholic Church,

the communion of saints,
the forgiveness of sins,
the resurrection of the body,
and the life everlasting.
Amen.

3 A CREED APPROVED BY THE UNITED CHURCH OF CANADA

We are not alone, we live in God's world.
We believe in God:
who has created and is creating,
who has come in Jesus, the Word made flesh,
to reconcile and make new,
who works in us and others by the Spirit.

We trust in God.

We are called to be the Church:
to celebrate God's presence,
to love and serve others,
to seek justice and resist evil,
to proclaim Jesus, crucified and risen,
our judge and our hope.

In life, in death, in life beyond death,
God is with us.
We are not alone.
Thanks be to God.

4 OUR SOCIAL CREED

We believe in God, Creator of the world;
and in Jesus Christ the Redeemer of creation.
We believe in the Holy Spirit,
through whom we acknowledge God's gifts,
and we repent of our sin
in misusing these gifts to idolatrous ends.

We affirm the natural world as God's handiwork
and dedicate ourselves to its preservation,
enhancement, and faithful use by humankind.

We joyfully receive, for ourselves and others,
the blessings of community, sexuality,
marriage, and the family.

We commit ourselves to the rights of men, women,
children, youth, young adults, the aging,
and those with handicapping conditions;
to improvement of the quality of life;
and to the rights and dignity
of racial, ethnic, and religious minorities.

We believe in the right and duty of persons
to work for the good of themselves and others,
and in the protection of their welfare in so doing;
in the rights to property as a trust from God,
collective bargaining, and responsible consumption;
and in the elimination of economic and social distress.

We dedicate ourselves to peace throughout the world, to
freedom for all peoples,
and to the rule of justice and law among nations.

We believe in the present and future triumph
of God's Word in human affairs,
and gladly accept our commission
to manifest the life of the gospel in the world.
Amen.

Litanies of Intercession

1

Let us pray for the Church and for the world.

Grant, Almighty God, that all who confess your Name may be
united in your truth, live together in your love, and reveal your
glory in the world. *Silence.* Lord, in your mercy

hear our prayer.

Guide the people of this land, and of all the nations, in the ways of justice and peace; that we may honor one another and serve the common good. *Silence.* Lord, in your mercy

hear our prayer.

Give us all a reverence for the earth as your own creation, that we may use its resources rightly in the service of others and to your honor and glory. *Silence.* Lord, in your mercy

hear our prayer.

Bless all whose lives are closely linked with ours, and grant that we may serve Christ in them, and love one another as he loves us. *Silence.* Lord, in your mercy

hear our prayer.

Comfort and heal all those who suffer in body, mind, or spirit; give them courage and hope in their troubles, and bring them the joy of your salvation. *Silence.* Lord, in your mercy

hear our prayer.

We commend to your mercy all who have died, that your will for them may be fulfilled; and we pray that we may share with all your saints in your eternal kingdom. *Silence.* Lord, in your mercy

hear our prayer. For the kingdom, the power, and the glory are yours, now and for ever. Amen.

2

Let us pray:

That the world may live in peace, and that the Church may achieve unity, fulfilling its service here and everywhere:

Lord, hear our prayer.

That all ministers and teachers in the Church may be faithful servants of the gospel, leading others into its way of life and strengthening their faith:

Lord, hear our prayer.

That the leaders of this nation and of the world may govern with justice and mercy, that all peoples may be freed from oppression and bondage, and that poverty may cease:

Lord, hear our prayer.

That all our work may be done for the common good, that it may be available to the unemployed, that it may be done in safety, and that it may fulfill the gifts and needs of all people:

Lord, hear our prayer.

That those who work on frontiers of truth and those who enrich our lives with beauty and joy may be free to follow their vocations:

Lord, hear our prayer.

That those who suffer disease or loneliness or grief may be healed and comforted:

Lord, hear our prayer.

That those whom we have known and loved who have died in the faith may be a glorious memory to us and a source of renewed communion with all the saints:

Lord, hear our prayer. For the kingdom, the power, and the glory are yours, now and for ever. Amen.

Prayers of Confession

1

Merciful God,
we confess that often we have failed
to be an obedient church.
We have not done your will,
we have broken your law,
we have rebelled against your love,
we have not loved our neighbors, and
we have not heard the cry of the needy.

Forgive us, we pray.
Free us for joyful obedience,
through Jesus Christ our Lord. **Amen.**

2

Most merciful God,
we confess that we have sinned against you
in thought, word, and deed,
by what we have done,
and by what we have left undone.
We have not loved you with our whole heart;
we have not loved our neighbors as ourselves.
We are truly sorry and we humbly repent.
For the sake of your Son Jesus Christ,
have mercy on us and forgive us;
that we may delight in your will,
and walk in your ways,
to the glory of your Name. **Amen.**

3   *(When Communion is to follow)*

We do not presume to come to this your table,
merciful Lord, trusting in our own goodness,
but in your unfailing mercies.
We are not worthy that you should receive us,
but give your word and we shall be healed,
through Jesus Christ our Lord. **Amen.**

Words of Pardon

1

Minister to People:
Hear the good news:
"Christ died for us while we were yet sinners;
that proves God's love toward us."
In the name of Jesus Christ, you are forgiven!

People to Minister:
In the name of Jesus Christ, you are forgiven!

Minister and People:
Glory to God. Amen.

2

Hear the good news:
"Christ died for us while we were yet sinners;
that proves God's love toward us."
In the name of Jesus Christ, you are forgiven!

3

Almighty God have mercy on you,
forgive you all your sins
through our Lord Jesus Christ,
strengthen you in all goodness,
and by the power of the Holy Spirit
keep you in eternal life.

4

In the mercy of almighty God,
Jesus Christ was given to die for you,
and for his sake God forgives you all your sins.
To those who believe in Jesus Christ
he gives the power to become the children of God
and bestows on them the Holy Spirit.

Invitations to the Peace

1

Let us offer one another signs of reconciliation and love.

2

The peace of the Lord be with you always.
And also with you.

3

Christ our Lord calls all who love him
to live in peace with one another.
Therefore, let us offer one another
signs of reconciliation and love.

4   *(When Communion is to follow)*

Christ our Lord invites to his table
all who love him and who seek
to live in peace with one another.
Therefore, let us offer one another
signs of reconciliation and love.

The Lord's Prayer

1   COMMON TEXT (INTERNATIONAL CONSUL-TATION ON ENGLISH TEXTS), 1975

Our Father in heaven,
hallowed be your name,
your kingdom come,
your will be done, on earth as in heaven.
Give us today our daily bread.
Forgive us our sins
as we forgive those who sin against us.
Save us from the time of trial
and deliver us from evil.
For the kingdom, the power, and the glory are yours
now and for ever. **Amen.**

2   FROM THE RITUAL OF THE METHODIST CHURCH, 1964

Our Father, who art in heaven,
hallowed be thy name.
Thy kingdom come,
thy will be done on earth as it is in heaven.
Give us this day our daily bread.
And forgive us our trespasses,
as we forgive those who trespass against us.
And lead us not into temptation,
but deliver us from evil.
For thine is the kingdom, and the power,
and the glory, forever. **Amen.**

3 FROM THE RITUAL OF THE EVANGELICAL UNITED BRETHREN CHURCH, 1959

Our Father, who art in heaven,
hallowed be thy name;
thy kingdom come,
thy will be done, on earth as it is in heaven.
Give us this day our daily bread;
and forgive us our debts,
as we forgive our debtors;
and lead us not into temptation,
but deliver us from evil.
For thine is the kingdom and the power
and the glory, forever. **Amen.**

Prayers After Communion

1

Eternal God, we give thanks for this holy mystery
in which you have given yourself to us.
Grant that we may go into the world
in the strength of your Spirit,
to give ourselves for others,
in the name of Jesus Christ our Lord. **Amen.**

2

You have given yourself to us, Lord.
Now we give ourselves for others.
Your love has made us a new people;
as a people of love we will serve you with joy.
Your glory has filled our hearts;
help us to glorify you in all things. Amen.

3

Most loving God,
you have given us a share
in the one bread and the one cup

and made us one with Christ.
Help us to bring your salvation and joy
to all the world.
We ask this through Christ our Lord.
Amen.

4

Bountiful God, we give you thanks
that you have refreshed us at your table
by granting us the presence of Christ.
Strengthen our faith,
increase our love for one another,
and send us forth into the world,
in courage and peace,
rejoicing in the power of the Holy Spirit.
Amen.

Concerning the Calendar and Lectionary

The following Calendar and the Common Lectionary that goes with it have been developed during the years 1978-82 by these denominations working together through the Consultation on Common Texts and its North American Committee on Calendar and Lectionary: American Lutheran Church, Association of Evangelical Lutheran Churches, Anglican Church of Canada, Christian Church/Disciples of Christ, Episcopal Church, Evangelical Lutheran Church of Canada, Lutheran Church—Missouri Synod, Lutheran Church in America, Presbyterian Church (U.S.A.), Reformed Church of America, Roman Catholic Church in the United States and Canada, United Church of Canada, United Church of Christ, and The United Methodist Church.

The remarkable story of the development of the ecumenical Calendar and Lectionary has been told in *Word and Table* and *Seasons of the Gospel*. This Calendar and Lectionary, in various versions, is now widely used by Christians of many denominations around the world. Its particularly wide use by North American Christians of many denominations in recent years led to the widespread call for a common version of the Calendar and Lectionary that would eliminate the discrepancies between the various denominational versions and take account of widespread criticism of the way in which the Old Testament lessons were selected. This led to an ecumenical North American Consultation on the Calendar and Lectionary in 1978 and to the work that has followed.

The Common Calendar is based on the most ancient traditions regarding the Christian Year, as explained in

Seasons of the Gospel. It consists of two cycles—the Christmas Cycle and the Easter Cycle. Each cycle consists of a preparatory season (Advent and Lent), a festival season (Christmas and Easter), and an "ordinary time" of growth (Seasons after Epiphany and after Pentecost). While denominations today are not legislating one rigid seasonal color code, the most common ecumenical practice is to use purple for preparatory seasons, white for festival seasons, green for growth seasons, and red or white for special days where one or the other color is appropriate.

Many questions have been asked by persons who are accustomed to the seasons of Pentecost and Kingdomtide as set forth in *The Book of Worship*, and it is important that several matters be clarified.

1. Kingdomtide was originally proposed in 1937 in a book sponsored by the former Federal Council of Churches as a six-month season beginning the Sunday after Pentecost. This was later modified to a proposal for two three-month seasons, and it was in this latter form that The Methodist Church adopted it in *The Book of Worship*. No other denomination has a season of Kingdomtide, and it is clear from many consultations that no other denomination is going to do so.

2. The term Pentecost Season originally meant "the Great Fifty Days" from Easter through the Day of Pentecost, and both the traditional and the new lectionaries make it clear that the Great Fifty Days are the time to celebrate not only the risen Christ but also the Holy Spirit. It is only through the work of the Holy Spirit that we know the risen Christ, and the two cannot be separated. The Season *after* Pentecost is just that; it is *not* the Pentecost Season.

3. The focus and emphases of the Season after Pentecost are made evident by the readings in the Lectionary, as are the foci and emphases of every other season. The Gospel readings for the Season after Pentecost go in course through the teaching portions of Matthew (Year A), Mark (Year B),

and Luke (Year C), in which Jesus' teaching about the Kingdom of God is clearly central. This theme is sounded with particular strength on the last few Sundays after Pentecost and reaches a climax on the last Sunday, which is called Christ the King. Thus, although the Common Calendar does not use the *term* "Kingdomtide," we have after Pentecost a season that fully serves the purposes intended for Kingdomtide.

The Calendar

ADVENT SEASON

First Sunday of Advent
  to Fourth Sunday of Advent

CHRISTMAS SEASON

Christmas Eve/Day
First Sunday after Christmas
New Year's Eve/Day

[Second Sunday after Christmas]
Epiphany

SEASON AFTER EPIPHANY

First Sunday after Epiphany
  (Baptism of the Lord)
Second Sunday after Epiphany
  to Eighth Sunday after
  Epiphany
Last Sunday after Epiphany
  (Transfiguration Sunday)

LENTEN SEASON

Ash Wednesday
First Sunday of Lent
  to Fifth Sunday of Lent
Holy Week
  Passion/Palm Sunday
  Monday in Holy Week
  Tuesday in Holy Week
  Wednesday in Holy Week
  Holy Thursday
  Good Friday
  Holy Saturday

EASTER SEASON

Easter Vigil
Easter
Second Sunday of Easter
  to Sixth Sunday of Easter
Ascension
  (Sixth Thursday of Easter)
Seventh Sunday of Easter
Pentecost

SEASON AFTER PENTECOST
(UNITED METHODIST KINGDOMTIDE)

Trinity Sunday (First
  Sunday after Pentecost)
Second Sunday
  after Pentecost to
  Twenty-seventh Sunday
  after Pentecost*
All Saints (Nov. 1 or
  First Sunday in Nov.)
Thanksgiving Day
Christ the King (Last
  Sunday after Pentecost)

*Lectionary readings on these Sundays are determined not by which Sunday it is after Pentecost but by the dates within which a Sunday falls.

Concerning Services of the Baptismal Covenant

The Sacrament of Holy Baptism is based upon God's covenant with the Church through the saving work of Jesus Christ and is the initiation service into Christ's holy Church. Persons baptized in infancy affirm this covenant for themselves in the rite of Confirmation. From time to time persons and congregations have occasion to reaffirm this covenant.

Closely related are the acts of reception into The United Methodist Church as a society within Christ's holy Church and reception into a local congregation.

While these are all distinct rites of the highest importance in themselves, there are two considerations that lead us to consider them together and submit a service text that can be used for any one or any combination of these rites.

1. They are all based on the baptismal covenant.

2. In practice it is common for two or more of these rites to be celebrated on a given occasion, and when these rites are printed separately the result can be needless duplication or confusion in trying to combine them. For example, a family seeking membership in a local church may consist of: (a) a mother being received by transfer from another United Methodist Church; (b) a father being received from membership in another denomination; (c) a child who has been baptized as an infant and is now ready to be confirmed; and (d) a child who is to be baptized. Each of these persons is taking a different step (or combination of steps), yet the family is being received by that congregation together at one time and place. Likewise, a confirmation class often contains both baptized and unbaptized members.

On any given occasion, the minister may find that the entire service is appropriate or that some parts of the service do not apply and should be omitted. When only infants are being baptized, for instance, those questions that apply only to candidates old enough to answer for themselves are of course omitted. When a class that includes no unbaptized persons is being confirmed, then of course the acts that relate only to Baptism are omitted. When a congregation is renewing its covenant (as on Watchnight), there may be no baptisms or confirmations to include. So many combinations of these rites may occur in the life of a congregation that it is not feasible to list them all and specify what must be done when; it is hoped that the service is sufficiently self-explanatory that decisions can be made by common sense.

It is hoped that these services, preceded by careful instruction, will help all who participate to know more fully the power of the gospel and the depth of commitment to which we are called in response.

The Baptismal Covenant:

Holy Baptism
Confirmation
Reaffirmation of Faith
Reception into The United Methodist Church
Reception into a Local Congregation

This is to be included where possible in a service of public worship, preferably as a response to the proclamation of the Word. Such parts as are not called for on a given occasion are to be omitted.

INTRODUCTION TO THE SERVICE

The minister makes such of the following statements to the congregation as may be appropriate:

Brothers and sisters in Christ:

Through the Sacrament of Baptism,
believers and their households
are initiated into Christ's holy Church.
We are incorporated into God's mighty acts of salvation
and given new birth through water and the Spirit.
All this is God's gift, offered to us without price.

Through Confirmation,
and through the reaffirmation of our faith,
we renew the covenant declared at our Baptism,
acknowledge what God is doing for us,
and affirm our commitment to Christ's holy Church.

PRESENTATION OF CANDIDATES

A representative of the congregation presents the candidates:

I present *Name(s)* for Baptism.
I present *Name(s)* for Confirmation.
I present *Name(s)* to reaffirm *their* faith.
I present *Name(s)*, who come(s) to this congregation from the
_____ Church.

RENUNCIATION OF SIN AND PROFESSION OF FAITH

The minister addresses parents or other sponsors, and those candidates who can answer for themselves:

On behalf of the whole Church, I ask you:
Do you reject the spiritual forces of wickedness,
the evil powers of this world,
and the bondage of sin?

I do.

Do you accept the freedom and power God gives you
to resist evil, injustice, and oppression
in whatever forms they present themselves?

I do.

Do you confess Jesus Christ as your Savior,
put your whole trust in his grace,
and promise to serve him as your Lord,
in union with the Church which Christ has opened
to people of all ages, nations, and races?

I do.

The minister addresses parents or other sponsors of candidates not able to answer for themselves:

Will you nurture *these children (persons)*
in Christ's holy Church,
that by your teaching and example
they may be guided to respond to God's grace,
openly to profess their faith,
and to lead a Christian life?

I will.

The minister addresses candidates who can answer for themselves [and their sponsors]:

According to the grace given to you,
will you remain *faithful members* of Christ's holy Church

and serve as Christ's *representatives* in the world?
[And will you who sponsor *these candidates*
support and encourage *them* in their Christian life?]

I will.

The minister addresses the congregation:

Do you as Christ's body, the Church,
reaffirm both your rejection of sin
and your commitment to Christ?

We do.

Will you nurture one another in the Christian faith and life
and include *these persons* now before you in your care?

**With God's help we will proclaim the good news
and live according to the example of Christ.
We will surround these persons
with a community of love and forgiveness,
that they may grow in their trust of God
and be found faithful in their service to others.
We will pray for them,
that they may be true disciples
who walk in the way that leads to life.**

The minister addresses the candidates and congregation:

Let us join together in professing the Christian faith as
contained in the Scriptures of the Old and New Testaments.

Do you believe in God the Father?

**I believe in God, the Father almighty,
creator of heaven and earth.**

Do you believe in Jesus Christ?

**I believe in Jesus Christ, his only Son, our Lord.
[He was conceived by the power of the Holy Spirit
and was born of the Virgin Mary.
He suffered under Pontius Pilate,
was crucified, died, and was buried.**

He descended to the dead.
On the third day he rose again.
He ascended into heaven,
and is seated at the right hand of the Father.
He will come again
to judge the living and the dead.]

Do you believe in the Holy Spirit?

I believe in the Holy Spirit,
[the holy catholic Church,
the communion of saints,
the forgiveness of sins,
the resurrection of the body,
and the life everlasting].

THANKSGIVING OVER THE WATER

Water may be poured into the font at this time.

The Lord be with you.

And also with you.

Let us pray.

Eternal Father:
When nothing existed but chaos
you swept across the dark waters
and brought forth light.
In the days of Noah
you saved those on the ark through water.
After the Flood you set in the clouds a rainbow.
When you saw your people as slaves in Egypt,
you led them to freedom through the sea.
Their children you brought through the Jordan
to the land which you promised.

Sing to the Lord all the earth.
Tell of God's mercy each day.

In the fullness of time you sent Jesus,
nurtured in the water of a womb.

He was baptized by John
and anointed by your Spirit.
He called his disciples
to share in the baptism of his death and resurrection
and to make disciples of all nations.

**Declare his works to the nations,
his glory among all the people.**

Pour out your Holy Spirit,
to bless this gift of water and those who receive it,
to wash away their sin
and clothe them in righteousness
throughout their lives,
that, dying and being raised with Christ,
they may share in his final victory.

**All praise to you, Eternal Father,
through your Son, Jesus Christ,
who with you and the Holy Spirit
lives and reigns for ever.
Amen.**

BAPTISM WITH LAYING ON OF HANDS

As each candidate is baptized, the minister says:

Name, I baptize you in the name of the Father,
and of the Son,
and of the Holy Spirit.

Amen.

*Immediately after the administration of the water, as hands are
placed on the head of each person by the minister and by others if
desired, the minister says to each:*

The Holy Spirit work within you,
that being born through water and the Spirit
you may be a faithful disciple of Jesus Christ.

Amen.

When all the candidates have been baptized, the congregation says to them:

Through Baptism
you are incorporated by the Holy Spirit
into God's new creation
and made to share in Christ's royal priesthood.
We are all one in Christ Jesus.
With joy and thanksgiving we welcome you
as *members* of the family of Christ.

CONFIRMATION OR REAFFIRMATION OF FAITH

Water may be sprinkled toward those being confirmed or reaffirming their faith, or the entire congregation when there is a congregational reaffirmation of the baptismal covenant.

The minister says:

Remember your Baptism and be thankful.

Amen.

As hands are placed on the head of each person being confirmed or reaffirming faith, by the minister and by others if desired, the minister says to each:

Name, the Holy Spirit work within you,
that having been born through water and the Spirit,
you may live as a faithful disciple of Jesus Christ.

Amen.

PROFESSION OR RENEWAL OF MEMBERSHIP IN THE UNITED METHODIST CHURCH

If there are persons coming into membership in The United Methodist Church who have not yet been presented, they may be presented at this time.

The minister addresses all those coming into membership in The United Methodist Church, or who have just professed or reaffirmed their faith within The United Methodist Church:

As *members* of Christ's universal Church,
will you be loyal to The United Methodist Church,
and do all in your power to strengthen its ministries?

I will.

*If there are persons joining this congregation from other United
Methodist congregations who have not yet been presented, they may
be presented at this time.*

*The minister addresses all those coming into membership in the
congregation, or who have just professed or reaffirmed their faith
within the congregation:*

As *members* of this congregation,
will you faithfully participate in its ministries
by your prayers, your presence,
your gifts, and your service?

I will.

COMMENDATION AND WELCOME

The minister addresses the congregation:

Members of the household of God,
I commend *these persons* to your love and care.
Do all in your power to increase *their* faith,
confirm *their* hope,
and perfect *them* in love.

The congregation responds:

**We give thanks
for all that God has already given you
and welcome you in Christian love.
As members together with you
in the body of Christ
and in this congregation
of The United Methodist Church,
we renew our covenant
faithfully to participate**

in the ministries of the Church
by our prayers, our presence,
our gifts, and our service,
that in everything God may be glorified
through Jesus Christ.

The minister addresses those newly received:

The God of all grace,
who has called us to eternal glory in Christ,
establish and strengthen you
by the power of the Holy Spirit,
that you may live in grace and peace.

One or more lay members may join with the minister in acts and words of welcome and peace.

Appropriate thanksgivings and intercessions for those who have participated in these acts should be included in the concerns and prayers which follow.

It is most fitting that the service conclude with Holy Communion, in which the union of the new members with the body of Christ is most fully expressed. The new members may receive first.

Concerning a Service of Christian Marriage

This service of Christian marriage is distinctive in several important respects.

1. It sets the marriage rite in the context of a full service of Christian worship, including the proclamation of the Word as well as prayer and praise. The service is parallel in its structure to the Sunday service, and Christian marriage is proclaimed as a sacred covenant reflecting Christ's covenant with his Church. Everything about the service is designed to witness that this is a *Christian* marriage.

2. Both words and actions consistently reflect the belief that husband and wife are equal partners in Christian marriage and that they who are entering into the marriage are doing so of their own volition.

3. Those present are to be an active congregation rather than simply passive witnesses. They give their blessing to the couple and to the marriage, they join in prayer and praise, and if there is Holy Communion they are invited to join with the couple in the Sacrament.

4. The service may or may not include Holy Communion. If Holy Communion is to be celebrated, it is most important that its significance be understood and made clear. Specifically: (a) Holy Communion is not being included as a part of the marriage rite; rather, the marriage rite is being included in a Christian Service of the Word and Holy Communion; (b) The Christian commitment of the participants is to be such that the Sacrament can be celebrated with integrity; (c) Not only the husband and wife but the whole congregation are to be invited to receive Communion. It is contrary to our tradition to celebrate the Holy Communion without an open invitation. On the other hand, there should be no pressure that would embarrass those who for whatever reason do not choose to receive Communion.

It should be clear that this service is not suited for every marriage occasion. It is important that the minister, in consultation with each couple, reach a responsible decision as to whether this service or some other marriage rite is most appropriate. Many people, however, have expressed a need for a service such as this; and it is hoped that it will be used widely to the glory of God and the celebration of Christian marriage.

A Service of Christian Marriage
The Entrance
GATHERING

While the people gather, instrumental or vocal music may be offered.

During the entrance of the wedding party, there may be instrumental music, or a hymn, a psalm, a canticle, or an anthem.

GREETING

Minister to people:

Friends, we are gathered together in the sight of God to witness and to bless the joining together of *Name* and *Name* in Christian marriage. The covenant of marriage was established by God, who created us male and female for each other. With his presence and power, Jesus graced a wedding at Cana of Galilee and in his sacrificial love gave us the example for the love of husband and wife. *Name* and *Name* come to give themselves to one another in this holy covenant.

Declaration of Intention

Minister to the persons who are to marry:

I ask you now
in the presence of God and these people
to declare your intention
to enter into union with one another
through the grace of Jesus Christ,
who has called you into union with himself
through baptism.

Minister to the woman:

Name, will you have *Name* to be your husband,
to live together in holy marriage?
Will you love him, comfort him, honor and keep him

in sickness and in health,
and forsaking all others, be faithful to him
as long as you both shall live?

Woman:

I will.

Minister to the man:

Name, will you have *Name* to be your wife,
to live together in holy marriage?
Will you love her, comfort her, honor and keep her
in sickness and in health,
and forsaking all others, be faithful to her
as long as you both shall live?

Man:

I will.

THE RESPONSE OF THE FAMILIES AND PEOPLE

Minister to people:

The marriage of *Name* and *Name* unites two families
and creates a new one.
They ask for your blessing.

Parents or other representatives of the families, if present, may respond:

We rejoice in your union,
and pray God's blessing upon you.

Minister to people:

Will all of you, by God's grace,
do everything in your power
to uphold and care for these two persons
in their marriage?

People:

We will.

PRAYER

Minister to people: The Lord be with you.

People: **And also with you.**

Minister:

Let us pray.
God of all peoples:
You are the true light illumining everyone.
You show us the way, the truth, and the life.
You love us even when we are disobedient.
You sustain us with your Holy Spirit.
We rejoice in your life in the midst of our lives.
We praise you for your presence with us,
and especially in this act of solemn covenant.
Through Jesus Christ our Lord.
Amen.

Proclamation and Response

One or more Scripture lessons are read.

A hymn, psalm, canticle, anthem, or other music may be offered before or after readings.

A sermon or other witness to Christian marriage is given.

Extemporaneous intercessory prayer may be offered, or the following may be prayed by the minister or by all:

Let us pray.
Eternal God,
creator and preserver of all life,
author of salvation, giver of all grace:
Bless and sanctify with your Holy Spirit
Name and *Name* who come now to join in marriage.
Grant that they may give their vows to each other
in the strength of your steadfast love.
Enable them to grow in love and peace
with you and with one another all their days,

that they may reach out
in concern and service to the world,
through Jesus Christ our Lord. **Amen.**

The Marriage

EXCHANGE OF VOWS

The woman and man face each other, joining hands.
Man to woman:

In the name of God,
I, Name, take you, Name,
to be my wife,
to have and to hold
from this day forward,
for better for worse,
for richer for poorer,
in sickness and in health,
to love and to cherish,
until we are parted by death.
This is my solemn vow.

Woman to man:

In the name of God,
I, Name, take you, Name,
to be my husband,
to have and to hold
from this day forward,
for better for worse,
for richer for poorer,
in sickness and in health,
to love and to cherish,
until we are parted by death.
This is my solemn vow.

BLESSING AND EXCHANGE OF RINGS

The minister may say:

These rings *(symbols)*
are the outward and visible sign

of an inward and spiritual grace,
signifying to us the union
between Jesus Christ and his Church.

The minister may bless the giving of rings or other symbols of the marriage.

Bless, O Lord, the giving of these rings *(symbols),*
that they who wear them may live in your peace,
and continue in your favor all the days of their life,
through Jesus Christ our Lord. **Amen.**

The giver(s) may say to the recipient(s):

**Name, I give you this ring *(symbol)*
as a sign of my vow,
and with all that I am,
and all that I have,
I honor you
in the name of the Father,
and of the Son,
and of the Holy Spirit.**

DECLARATION OF MARRIAGE

The wife and husband join hands. The minister may place a hand on, or wrap a stole around, their joined hands.

Minister to husband and wife:

You have declared your consent and vows
before God and this congregation.
May God confirm your covenant
and fill you both with grace.

Minister to people:

Now that *Name* and *Name*
have given themselves to each other by solemn vows,
with the joining of hands,
and the giving and receiving of *rings,*
I announce to you that they are husband and wife
in the name of the Father, and of the Son,
and of the Holy Spirit.

Those whom God has joined together,
let no one put asunder.

People: **Amen.**

A doxology or other hymn may be sung.

Intercessions may be offered for the Church and for the world.

BLESSING OF THE MARRIAGE

The husband and wife may kneel, as the minister prays:

O God,
you have so consecrated the
covenant of Christian marriage
that in it is represented
the covenant between Christ and his Church.
Send therefore your blessing upon *Name* and *Name,*
that they may surely keep their marriage covenant
and so grow in love and godliness together,
that their home may be a haven
of blessing and peace,
through Jesus Christ our Lord.

Amen.

If Holy Communion is not to be celebrated, the service continues with the Lord's Prayer and concludes with the Sending Forth.

Thanksgiving and Communion

TAKING THE BREAD AND CUP

Minister to people:

Let us offer ourselves and our gifts to God.

Here the husband and wife or representatives of the congregation may bring the bread and wine to the Lord's table. The minister takes them and prepares them for the meal.

THE GREAT THANKSGIVING

The Lord be with you.

And also with you.

Lift up your hearts.

We lift them to the Lord.

Let us give thanks to the Lord our God.

It is right to give our thanks and praise.

It is right, and a good and joyful thing,
always and everywhere to give thanks to you,
Father Almighty, Creator of heaven and earth.
You formed us in your image,
male and female you created us.
You gave us the gift of marriage,
that we might fulfill one another.
And so,
with your people on earth and all the company of heaven
we praise your name and join their unending hymn:

Holy, holy, holy Lord, God of power and might,
heaven and earth are full of your glory.
Hosanna in the highest.
Blessed is he who comes in the name of the Lord.
Hosanna in the highest.

Holy are you, and blessed is your Son Jesus Christ.
By the baptism
of his suffering, death, and resurrection
you gave birth to your Church,
delivered us from slavery to sin and death,
and made with us a new covenant
by water and the Spirit,
from which flows the covenant love
of husband and wife.

On the night in which he gave himself up for us
he took bread, gave thanks to you, broke the bread,
gave it to his disciples, and said:
"Take, eat; this is my body which is given for you.
Do this in remembrance of me."

When the supper was over he took the cup,
gave thanks to you, gave it to his disciples, and said:
"Drink from this, all of you;
this is my blood of the new covenant,
poured out for you and for many
for the forgiveness of sins.
Do this, as often as you drink it,
in remembrance of me.

And so,
in remembrance of these your mighty acts
in Jesus Christ,
we offer ourselves in praise and thanksgiving
as a holy and living sacrifice,
in union with Christ's offering for us,
as we proclaim the mystery of faith.

Christ has died, Christ is risen, Christ will come again.

Pour out your Holy Spirit on us, gathered here,
and on these gifts of bread and wine.
Make them be for us the body and blood of Christ,
that we may be for the world the body of Christ,
redeemed by his blood.

By the same Spirit bless *Name* and *Name*,
that their love for each other
may reflect the love of Christ for us
and grow from strength to strength
as they faithfully serve you in the world.
Finally, by your grace,
bring them and all of us to that table
where your saints feast forever
in your heavenly home.

Through your Son Jesus Christ,
with the Holy Spirit in your holy Church,
all honor and glory is yours, Almighty Father,
now and for ever.
Amen.

And now, with the confidence of children of God, let us pray:

All pray the Lord's Prayer.

BREAKING THE BREAD

The minister breaks the bread and then lifts the cup, in silence or with appropriate words.

GIVING THE BREAD AND CUP

The bread and wine are given to the people, with these or other words being exchanged:

The body of Christ, given for you. **Amen.**
The blood of Christ, given for you. **Amen.**

Sending Forth

Here may be a hymn or Psalm 128.

DISMISSAL WITH BLESSING

God the Eternal keep you in love with each other,
so that the peace of Christ may abide in your home.
Go to serve God and your neighbor in all that you do.

Bear witness to the love of God in this world
so that those to whom love is a stranger
will find in you generous friends.
The grace of the Lord Jesus Christ,
and the love of God,
and the communion of the Holy Spirit be with you all.
Amen.

THE PEACE

The peace of the Lord be with you always.

And also with you.

The couple and minister(s) may greet each other, after which greetings may be exchanged throughout the congregation.

GOING FORTH

A hymn may be sung or instrumental music played as the couple, the wedding party, and the people leave.

Concerning a Service of Death and Resurrection

The service should properly be held in the church if at all possible, and at a time when members of the congregation can be present.

The pastor should be notified immediately of the death of a member or associate of the congregation. Whenever the pastor's service or the use of the church building is desired, arrangements should be made and approved in consultation with the pastor.

This order is intended for use with the body of the deceased present, but it can be adapted for use at memorial services or other occasions.

The coffin remains closed throughout the service and thereafter. It may be covered with a pall.

Members of the deceased's family, friends, and members of the congregation are encouraged strongly to share in conducting the service.

Use of the term "Service of Death and Resurrection" is not intended to discourage the use of the more familiar terms "funeral," "burial of the dead," or "memorial service." The term "funeral" is appropriate for a service with the body of the deceased present. The term "burial of the dead" is appropriate for a service where the remains of the deceased are buried. The term "memorial service" is appropriate where the body of the deceased is not present. Since the service here presented is adaptable for use in a wide variety of situations, it was felt that a more comprehensive title was needed. The term "Service of Death and Resurrection" is not only appropriate to any situation in which this service might be used, it expresses clearly the twofold nature of what is done: the facts of death and bereavement are honestly faced, and the gospel of resurrection is celebrated in the context of God's covenant with us in Christ.

A Service of Death and Resurrection

The Entrance

GATHERING

The minister may greet the family.

Music for worship may be offered while the people gather.

Hymns and songs of faith may be sung during the gathering.

The pall may be placed on the coffin with these words:

Dying, Christ destroyed our death.
Rising, Christ restored our life.
Christ will come again in glory.
As in baptism *Name* put on Christ,
so in Christ may *Name* be clothed with glory.
Here and now, dear friends, we are God's children.
What we shall be has not yet been revealed.
But we know that when he appears we shall be like him,
for we shall see him as he is.
Those who have this hope purify themselves
as Christ is pure.

The coffin then may be carried into the place of worship in procession, the minister going before it and saying the Word of Grace, the congregation standing. Or, if the coffin is already in place, the minister says the following from a place in front of the congregation.

THE WORD OF GRACE

Jesus said, I am the Resurrection and I am Life.
Those who believe in me, even though they die,
yet shall they live,
and whoever lives and believes in me shall never die.
I am Alpha and Omega,
the beginning and the end, the first and the last.
I died, and behold I am alive forever more,
and I hold the keys of hell and death.
Because I live, you shall live also.

GREETING

Friends, we have gathered here to praise God
and to witness to our faith
as we celebrate the life of *Name*.
We come together in grief
acknowledging our human loss.
May God grant us grace,
that in pain we may find comfort,
in sorrow hope, in death resurrection.

*If a pall was not placed on the coffin earlier, the sentences used above
for that act may be added here instead.*

HYMN OR SONG

PRAYER

*The following or other prayers may be offered, in unison if desired.
Petition for God's help, thanksgiving for the communion of saints,
confession of sin, and assurance of pardon are appropriate here.*

The Lord be with you.

And also with you.

Let us pray. *(together the Opening Prayer)*

**O God, who gave us birth,
You are ever more ready to hear
than we are to pray.
You know our needs before we ask,
and our ignorance in asking.
Give to us now your grace,
that as we shrink before the mystery of death
we may see the light of eternity.
Speak to us once more
your solemn message of life and of death.
Help us to live as those who are prepared to die.
And when our days here are accomplished,
enable us to die as those who go forth to live,
so that living or dying, our life may be in you,**

and that nothing in life or in death
be able to separate us
from your great love in Christ Jesus our Lord. Amen.

and/or

Eternal God, we praise you for the great company
of all those who have finished their course in faith
and now rest from their labor.

We praise you for those dear to us
whom we name in our hearts before you.
Especially we praise you for *Name*,
whom you have graciously received
into your presence.
To all of these, grant your peace.
Let perpetual light shine upon them;
and help us so to believe where we have not seen,
that your presence may lead us through our years,
and bring us at last with them
into the joy of your home
not made with hands but eternal in the heavens;
through Jesus Christ our Lord. Amen.

The following prayer of confession and pardon may also be used.

Holy God, before you our hearts are open
and from you no secrets are hidden.
We bring to you now
our shame and sorrow for our sins.
We have forgotten
that our life is from you and unto you.
We have neither sought nor done your will.
We have not been truthful in our hearts,
in our speech, in our lives.
We have not loved as we ought to love.
Help us and heal us,
raising us from our sins into a better life,
that we may end our days in peace,

trusting in your kindness unto the end;
through Jesus Christ our Lord,
who lives and reigns with you
in the unity of the Holy Spirit,
one God now and for ever. Amen.

Who is in a position to condemn?
Only Christ, Christ who died for us, who rose for us,
who reigns at God's right hand and prays for us.
Thanks be to God who gives us the victory
through our Lord Jesus Christ.

PSALM 130

Out of the depths I cry unto thee, O Lord!
Lord, hear my cry.
Let thine ears be attentive
to the voice of my supplication.
If thou, Lord, should mark iniquities,
Lord, who could stand?
But there is forgiveness with thee,
that thou may be feared
I wait for the Lord, my soul waits,
and in his word do I hope.
My soul waits for the Lord
more than those who watch for the morning.
O Israel, hope in the Lord!
For with the Lord is great mercy.
With him is plenteous redemption,
and he will redeem Israel from all their sins.

Proclamation and Response

OLD TESTAMENT LESSON

Arrangement of verses may be altered.

Preferred:

Isaiah 40:1-6, 8-11, 28-31

Recommended:

Exodus 14:5-14, 19-31
Isaiah 43:1-3*a*, 5-7, 13, 15, 18-19, 25; 44:6, 8*a*
Isaiah 55:1-3, 6-13

PSALM 23

Sung or said by the people, standing.

The Lord is my shepherd; I shall not want.
He maketh me to lie down in green pastures:
he leadeth me beside the still waters.
He restoreth my soul:
he leadeth me in the paths of righteousness
for his name's sake.
Yea, though I walk
through the valley of the shadow of death
I will fear no evil:
for thou art with me;
thy rod and thy staff they comfort me.
Thou preparest a table before me
in the presence of mine enemies;
thou anointest my head with oil;
my cup runneth over.
Surely goodness and mercy shall follow me
all the days of my life:
and I will dwell in the house of the Lord for ever.

NEW TESTAMENT LESSON

Arrangement of verses may be altered.

Preferred:
1 Corinthians 15:1-8, 12-20, 35-44, 53-55, 57-58
Revelation 21:1-7, 22-27; 22:1-5

Recommended:
Romans 8:1-2, 5-6, 10-11, 14-19, 22-28, 31-32, 35-39
2 Corinthians 4:5-18
Ephesians 1:15-23; 2:1, 4-10
1 Peter 1:3-9, 13, 21-25
Revelation 7:2-3, 9-17

PSALM OR HYMN

Recommended, either here or after the Old Testament Lesson:
Psalm 42, 43, 46, 90, 91, 103, 116, 121, 139, 145, 146

GOSPEL LESSON

Arrangement of verses may be altered.

Preferred:
John 14:1-10a, 15-21, 25-27

Recommended:
Luke 24:13-35
John 11:1-5, 20-27, 32-35, 38-44

SERMON

A sermon may be preached, proclaiming the gospel in the face of death. It may lead into, or include, the following acts of naming and witness.

NAMING

The life and death of the deceased may be gathered up by the reading of a memorial or appropriate statement, or in other ways, by the pastor or others.

WITNESS

Family, friends, and members of the congregation may briefly voice their thankfulness to God for the grace they have received in the life of the deceased and their Christian faith and joy. Signs of faith, hope, and love may be exchanged.

HYMN OR SONG

CREED

The congregation, standing, may be led in the Apostles' Creed.

I believe in God, the Father almighty,
creator of heaven and earth.

I believe in Jesus Christ, his only Son, our Lord.
He was conceived by the power of the Holy Spirit
and born of the Virgin Mary.
He suffered under Pontius Pilate,
was crucified, died, and was buried.
He descended to the dead.
On the third day he rose again.
He ascended into heaven,
and is seated at the right hand of the Father.
He will come again to judge the living and the dead.

I believe in the Holy Spirit,
the holy catholic Church,
the communion of saints,
the forgiveness of sins,
the resurrection of the body,
and the life everlasting.
Amen.

If the Creed has not been preceded by, it may be followed by, a hymn or musical response.

The Commendation

If the Committal is to conclude this service, it may be shortened and substituted for the Commendation.

PRAYERS

One or more of the following prayers may be offered, or other prayers may be used. They may take the form of a pastoral prayer, a series of shorter prayers, or a litany. Intercession, commendation of life, and thanksgiving are appropriate here, concluded with the Lord's Prayer.

God of us all, your love never ends.
When all else fails, you still are God.
We pray to you for one another in our need,
and for all, anywhere, who mourn with us this day.
To those who doubt, give light;
to those who are weak, strength;
to all who have sinned, mercy;
to all who sorrow, your peace.
Keep true in us
the love with which we hold one another.
In all our ways we trust you.
And to you,
with your Church on earth and in heaven,
we offer honor and glory, now and for ever.
Amen.

O God, all that you have given us is yours.
As first you gave *Name* to us
so now we give *Name* back to you.
Here the minister, with others, standing near the coffin, may lay hands on it, continuing:
Receive *Name* into the arms of your mercy.
Raise *Name* up with all your people.
Receive us also, and raise us into a new life.
Help us so to love and serve you in this world
that we may enter into your joy in the world to come.
Amen.

Into your hands, O merciful Savior,
we commend your servant *Name.*

Acknowledge, we humbly beseech you,
a sheep of your own fold,
a lamb of your own flock,
a sinner of your own redeeming.
Receive *Name* into the arms of your mercy,
into the blessed rest of everlasting peace,
and into the glorious company of the saints of light.
Amen.

*The minister may administer the Holy Communion to all present
who wish to share at the Lord's Table, using An Order for Holy
Communion below. Otherwise, the service continues with the
following thanksgiving:*

God of love, we thank you
for all with which you have blessed us
even to this day:
for the gift of joy in days of health and strength,
and for the gifts of your abiding presence and promise
in days of pain and grief.
We praise you for home and friends,
and for our baptism and place in your Church
with all who have faithfully lived and died.
Above all else we thank you for Jesus,
who knew our griefs,
who died our death and rose for our sake,
and who lives and prays for us.
And as he taught us, so now we pray.

All pray the Lord's Prayer.
HYMN

Dismissal with Blessing

*The minister, facing the people, may give one or more of the
following, or other, words of dismissal with blessing.*

Now may the God of Peace
who brought again from the dead our Lord Jesus,

the great Shepherd of the sheep,
by the blood of the eternal covenant,
equip you with everything good
that you may do his will,
working in you that which is pleasing in his sight,
through Jesus Christ;
to whom be glory for ever and ever. **Amen.**

The peace of God which passes all understanding
keep your hearts and minds
in the knowledge and love of God,
and of his Son Jesus Christ our Lord.
And the blessing of God Almighty,
the Father, Son, and Holy Spirit,
be among you and remain with you always. **Amen.**

Now may the Father
from whom every family in heaven and on earth
is named,
according to the riches of his glory,
grant you to be strengthened with might
through his Spirit in your inner being,
that Christ may dwell in your hearts through faith;
that you, being rooted and grounded in love,
may be able to comprehend with all the saints
what is the breath and length and height and depth,
and to know the love of Christ
which surpasses knowledge,
that you may be filled with all the fullness of God.
Amen.

Now to the One who by the power at work within us
is able to do far more abundantly
than all that we ask or think,
to this God be glory in the Church
and in Christ Jesus
to all generations, for ever and ever. **Amen.**

An Order for Holy Communion

*This order may be included in the Service following the
Commendation, or before a common meal following the Service, or
with the family at some time following the Service. If included, it
replaces the thanksgiving, the Lord's Prayer, and the hymn at the
end of the Commendation.*

*The bread and wine are brought to the table, or uncovered if already
in place. The pastor makes any necessary preparation of the
elements and then prays the following or another version of the
Great Thanksgiving:*

The Lord be with you.

And also with you.

Lift up your hearts.

We lift them to the Lord.

Let us give thanks to the Lord our God.

It is right to give our thanks and praise.

It is right that we should always and everywhere
give thanks to you,
Father Almighty, Creator of heaven and earth,
through Jesus Christ our Lord,
who rose victorious from the dead
and comforts us
with the blessed hope of everlasting life.
And so,
with your people on earth
and all the company of heaven
we praise your name and join their unending hymn:

**Holy, holy, holy Lord, God of power and might,
heaven and earth are full of your glory.
Hosanna in the highest.
Blessed is he who comes in the name of the Lord.
Hosanna in the highest.**

Holy are you, and blessed is your Son Jesus Christ.
By the baptism of his suffering, death, and resurrection
you gave birth to your Church,
delivered us from slavery to sin and death,
and made with us a new covenant by water and the Spirit.
When the Lord Jesus ascended,
he promised to be with us always,
in the power of your Word and Holy Spirit.

On the night in which he gave himself up for us
he took bread, gave thanks to you, broke the bread,
gave it to his disciples, and said:
"Take, eat; this is my body which is given for you.
Do this in remembrance of me."

When the supper was over he took the cup,
gave thanks to you, gave it to his disciples, and said:
"Drink from this, all of you;
this is my blood of the new covenant,
poured out for you and for many
for the forgiveness of sins.
Do this, as often as you drink it, in remembrance of me."

And so,
in remembrance of these your mighty acts in Jesus Christ,
we offer ourselves in praise and thanksgiving
as a holy and living sacrifice,
in union with Christ's offering for us,
as we proclaim the mystery of faith.

Christ has died, Christ is risen, Christ will come again.

Pour out your Holy Spirit on us, gathered here,
and on these gifts of bread and wine.
Make them be for us the body and blood of Christ,
that we may be for the world the body of Christ,
redeemed by his blood.

By your Spirit make us one with Christ,
one with each other,

and one in communion with all your saints,
especially *Name* and all those most dear to us.
Finally, by your grace,
bring them and all of us to that table
where your saints feast forever in your heavenly home.

Through your Son Jesus Christ,
with the Holy Spirit in your holy Church,
all honor and glory is yours, Almighty Father,
now and for ever.

Amen.

And now, with the confidence of children of God,
let us pray:

All pray the Lord's Prayer.

*The minister breaks the bread and then lifts the cup, in silence or
with appropriate words.*

*The bread and wine are given to the people, with these or other
words being exchanged:*

The body of Christ, given for you. **Amen.**

The blood of Christ, given for you. **Amen.**

*During the giving of the bread and wine,
hymns or songs of praise may be sung.*

Then follows the Dismissal with Blessing.

An Order of Committal

*This order is intended primarily for burial in the ground. However,
it can be adapted for cremation or the interment of ashes, for burial
above ground or at sea, or when the body is donated for medical
purposes.*

The pastor should preside.

*Prayers and lections appropriate for a service for a child or youth, or
for other distinctive occasions, may be used instead of the following.*

When the people have gathered, one or more of the following are said:

In the midst of life we are in death;
from whom can we seek help?
Our help is in the name of the Lord,
who made heaven and earth.
He who raised Jesus Christ from the dead
will give life to your mortal bodies also
through his Spirit which dwells in you.

Behold, I tell you a mystery!
We shall not all die, but we shall all be changed.
This perishable nature must put on the imperishable,
this mortal the immortal.
Then shall come to pass the saying,
"Death is swallowed up in victory."
"O death, where is your sting?
O grave, where is your victory?"
Thanks be to God who gives us the victory
through our Lord Jesus Christ.

Therefore my heart is glad and my spirit rejoices.
My body also shall rest in hope.
You, Lord, will show me the path of life.
In your presence is fullness of joy.
At your right hand are pleasures forever more.

The following prayer is offered:

Let us pray.

O God, you have ordered this wonderful world
and know all things in earth and in heaven.
Give us such faith that by day and by night,
at all times and in all places,
we may without fear commit ourselves
and those dear to us
to your never-failing love,
in this life and in the life to come. **Amen.**

One of the following or other Scriptures may be read:

Blessed be the God and Father of our Lord Jesus Christ! By his great mercy we have been born anew to a living hope through the resurrection of Jesus Christ from the dead, and to an inheritance which is imperishable, undefiled and unfading, kept in heaven for you. In this you rejoice, though now for a little while you suffer trials so that the genuineness of your faith may prove itself worthy at the revelation of Jesus Christ. Without having seen him, yet you love him; though you do not now see him, you believe in him and rejoice with unutterable and exalted joy. As the harvest of your faith you reap the salvation of your souls.

Jesus said: Truly, truly, I say to you, unless a grain of wheat falls into the earth and dies, it remains alone; but if it dies it bears much fruit. He who loves his life loses it, and he who hates his life in this world will keep it for eternal life. If anyone serves me, he must follow me; and where I am, there shall my servant be also. If anyone serves me, the Father will honor him.

Standing at the head of the coffin and facing it, while earth is cast upon it as the coffin is lowered into the grave, the minister says the following:

Almighty God, into your hands we commend your child *Name*, in sure and certain hope of resurrection to eternal life through Jesus Christ our Lord. **Amen.**

This body we commit to the ground
(*or* the elements, *or* its resting place),
earth to earth, ashes to ashes, dust to dust.
Blessed are the dead who die in the Lord.
Henceforth, says the Spirit,
they rest from their labors
and their works do follow them.

One or more of the following or other prayers is offered:

Let us pray.

Gracious God,
we thank you for those we love but see no more.
Receive into your arms your servant *Name*,
and grant that increasing in knowledge and love of you,
he/she may go from strength to strength
in service to your heavenly kingdom;
through Jesus Christ our Lord. **Amen.**

Almighty God,
look with pity upon the sorrow of your servants,
for whom we pray.
Amidst things they cannot understand,
help them to trust in your care.
Bless them and keep them.
Make your face to shine upon them
and be gracious to them.
Lift up your countenance upon them
and give them peace. **Amen.**

O God, whose days are without end,
make us deeply aware of the shortness
and uncertainty of our human life.
Raise us from sin into love and goodness,
that when we depart this life we may rest in Christ
and receive the blessing he has promised
to those who love and serve him:
"Come, you blessed of my Father,
receive the kingdom
prepared for you from the foundation of the world."
Grant this, merciful Father,
through Jesus Christ our Mediator and Redeemer.
Amen.

O Lord, support us all the day long of our troubled life,
until the shadows lengthen and the evening comes,

and the busy world is hushed,
and the fever of life is over and our work is done.
Then in your mercy grant us a safe lodging,
and a holy rest, and peace at the last;
through Jesus Christ our Lord. **Amen.**

Eternal God, you have shared with us the life of *Name.*
Before *he/she* was ours, *he/she* is yours.
For all that *Name* has given us to make us what we are,
for that of *him/her* which lives and grows in each of us,
and for *his/her* life that in your love will never end,
we give you thanks.
As now we offer *Name* back into your arms,
comfort us in our loneliness,
strengthen us in our weakness,
and give us courage to face the future unafraid.
Draw those of us who remain in this life
closer to one another,
make us faithful to serve one another,
and give us to know that peace and joy
which is eternal life;
through Jesus Christ our Lord. **Amen.**

The Lord's Prayer may follow.

A hymn or song may be sung.

*The minister dismisses the people with the following or another
blessing:*

Now unto him who is able to keep you from falling,
and to present you faultless
before the presence of his glory
with exceeding joy,
to the only God our Savior
be glory and majesty, dominion and power,
through Jesus Christ our Lord,
both now and forever more. **Amen.**

Sources of Prayers for General Services

The texts of the Apostles' Creed, the Nicene Creed, the Sursum Corda, the Sanctus and Benedictus, and the Lord's Prayer are from *Prayers We Have in Common*, copyright © 1970, 1971, and 1975, International Consultation on English Texts.

The Acclamation is from the English translation of *The Roman Missal* © 1973, International Committee on English in the Liturgy, Inc. All rights reserved.

A SUNDAY SERVICE (Complete Text)

Opening Prayer—Text from (or, adapted from) *The Book of Common Prayer*, p. 355.

The Prayer for Illumination, the Confession and Pardon, and the Offering sentence are from *The Sacrament of the Lord's Supper: An Alternate Text 1972*.

GREETINGS

1. *We Gather Together*, p. 5.
2. *An Alternate Text 1972.*
3. International Consultation on English Texts.
4. Traditional.

OPENING PRAYERS

1. Text from (or, adapted from) *The Book of Common Prayer*, p. 355.
2. Adapted from *The Sacrament of the Lord's Supper: A New Text*, copyright © 1982 by the Consultation on Church Union, p. 1.
3. Freely adapted from *Seasons of the Gospel*, p. 82.

4. Susan J. and James F. White
5. *Lutheran Book of Worship*, pp. 57f. (alt.).

CREEDS

1. International Consultation on English Texts.
2. Ibid.
3. The United Church of Canada "Creed" is used by permission of the General Council of The United Church of Canada.
4. *The Book of Discipline* (1984), p. 104.

LITANIES OF INTERCESSION

1. Text from (or, adapted from) *The Book of Common Prayer*, p. 388.
2. *An Alternate Text 1972* (alt.).

PRAYERS OF CONFESSION

1. *An Alternate Text 1972.*
2. Text from (or, adapted from) *The Book of Common Prayer*, p. 360.
3. Freely adapted from *The Book of Common Prayer* and excerpts from the English translation of *The Roman Missal* © 1973, International Committee on English in the Liturgy, Inc. All rights reserved.

WORDS OF PARDON

1. *An Alternate Text 1972* (alt.).
2. Ibid.
3. Text from (or, adapted from) *The Book of Common Prayer*, p. 360.
4. Excerpts from the Lutheran Book of Worship, copyright © 1978. Reprinted by permission of Augsburg. Publishing House.

INVITATIONS TO THE PEACE

1. *An Alternate Text 1972.*
2. Text from (or, adapted from) *The Book of Common Prayer*, p. 360.

3. *We Gather Together,* p. 7 (alt.).
4. *An Alternate Text 1972* (alt.).

PRAYERS AFTER COMMUNION

1. Original.
2. *An Alternate Text 1972.*
3. Excerpts from the English translation of *The Roman Missal* © 1973, International Committee on English in the Liturgy, Inc. All rights reserved.
4. Adapted from *The Sacrament of the Lord's Supper: A New Text,* copyright © 1982 by the Consultation on Church Union, p. 5.

A SERVICE OF CHRISTIAN MARRIAGE

The texts of the declaration of intention, the marriage vows, the exchange of rings, the minister's announcement that the couple are husband and wife, and the blessing of the marriage are adapted from "The Celebration and Blessing of a Marriage" in *The Book of Common Prayer,* pp. 423 ff.

A SERVICE OF DEATH AND RESURRECTION

The third prayer in the Commendation is taken from (or, adapted from) *The Book of Common Prayer,* p. 499.